THeN THeI ꟷ VIOLet

Written and Illustrated by
Jamie L. Glaser

ISBN 978-1-530-70970-0

Published by
Jamie L. Glaser

Avery,
Dream Big!
Jamie Glaser

Oh girls,
You bring my life
joy,
laughter,
hope,
and
inspiration.
I love you all so much.

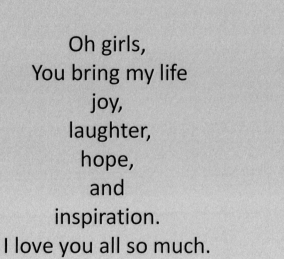

"Oooh girls…" calls Mom. "Dinner is almost ready. Come set the table." The girls dash to the kitchen with hungry grins.

Abbey gets the plates and cups.

Madie folds the napkins up.

Heidi goes to feed the pup.

And then...

There's Violet.

"Oh girls…" says Mom. "It's a beautiful night! Let's get some fresh air and play outside." The girls race to the backyard and into the warm summer night.

Madie's busy counting stars.

Abbey thinks she's spotted Mars.

Heidi's catching bugs in jars.

And then...

There's Violet.

"Oh girls!" exclaims Mom. "It's time to get ready for bed. Wash your hands and face please."

The girls meander to the bathroom to get ready for bed.
Abbey washes her face clean.
Madie brushes teeth that gleam.
Heidi flosses in between.

And then...

There's Violet.

"Ooooooh girls..." declares Mom. "It's story time. Come hear our new book!" The girls fly to the bedroom to find a cozy spot.

Abbey hugs her teddy bear.

Madie rests in a bean bag chair.

Heidi dreams of the castle square.

And then...

There's Violet.

"Oh Violet!" erupts Mom. "Dinner table and back yard mess, filthy hands and dirty dress, the doll and toothpaste, and now what's more? All your things are on the floor."

Mom sighs deeply and tucks the girls into their beds.
"Goodnight girls." whispers Mom. Soon Madie's falling fast
asleep.

Abbey doesn't make a peep.

Heidi rests while counting sheep.

And then...

There's Violet. "Sorry Mommy." says Violet. "We'll clean up in the morning." says Mom.

Made in the USA
San Bernardino, CA
23 April 2016